Salish Elders

MW01528827

Salish Elders

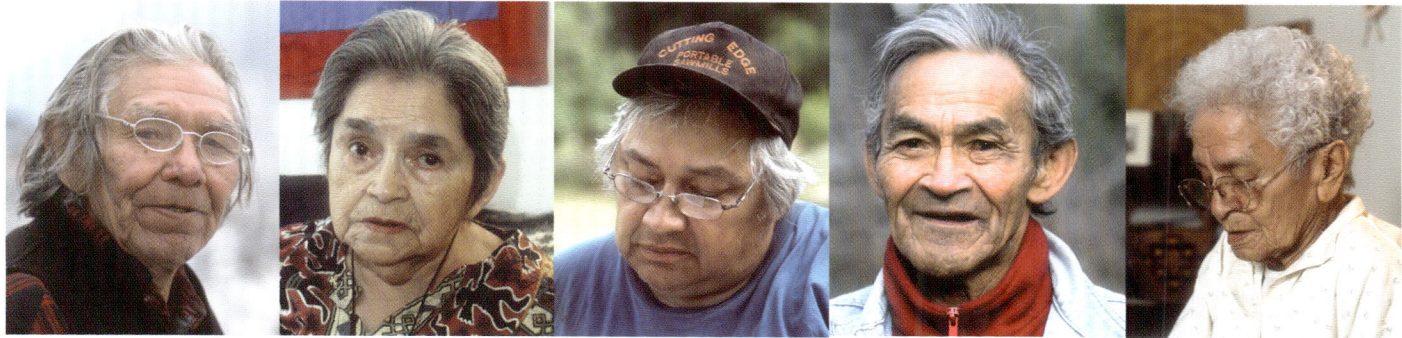

Portraits of Elders of the Interior Salish of British Columbia, Canada

WIM TEWINKEL

CAITLIN PRESS INC. 2003

Copyright © Wim Tewinkel 2003
All rights reserved. No part of this publication may be reproduced, stored in a retrieval system or transmitted, in any form or by any means, without the prior permission of the publisher, or in the case of photocopying or reprographic copying, a licence from Access Copyright, the Canadian Copyright Licensing Agency, 1 Yonge Street, Suite 1900, Toronto, Ontario, M5E 1E5, www.accesscopyright.ca, 1-800-893-5777, info@accesscopyright.

Published by
Caitlin Press Inc.
Box 2387
Prince George BC V2N 2S6

Design by Warren Clark/Wim Tewinkel
Typeset by Warren Clark Graphic Design

Caitlin Press acknowledges the financial support from Canada Council for the Arts and from British Columbia Arts Council for its publishing program.

National Library of Canada Cataloguing in Publication Data

Tewinkel, W. H., 1945-
    Salish Elders / W.H. Tewinkel

    ISBN 0-920576-98-2

    1. Salish Indians—Pictorial works. 2. Salish Indians—biography. I. Title.
E99.S2T48 2003   971.1'004979   C2003-910847-3

Contents

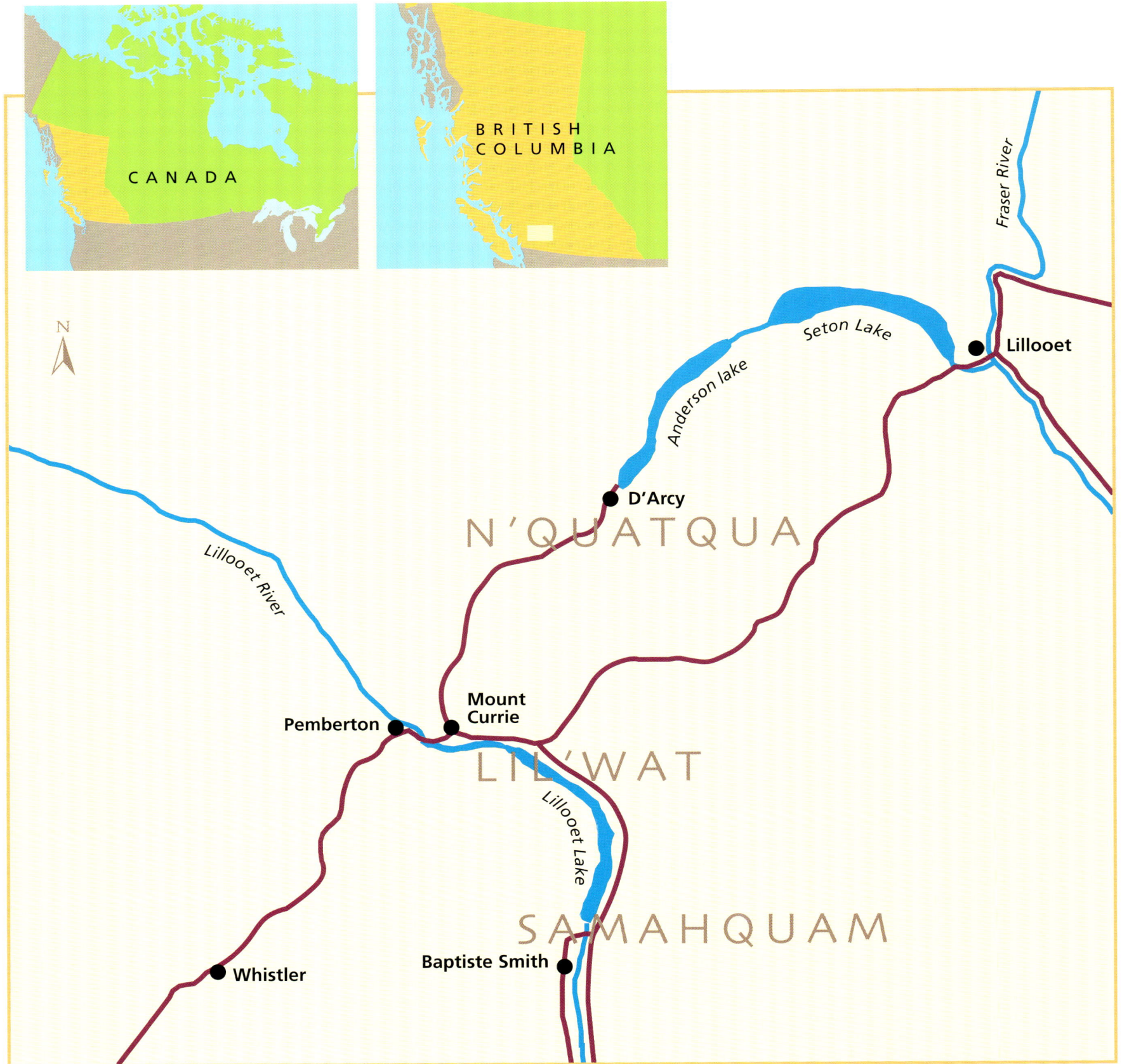

CANADA

BRITISH COLUMBIA

Fraser River

Seton Lake

Anderson lake

Lillooet

D'Arcy

N'QUATQUA

Lillooet River

Pemberton

Mount Currie

LIL'WAT

Lillooet Lake

SAMAHQUAM

Whistler

Baptiste Smith

Preface

The people presented in this book live in the mountains of British Columbia near Pemberton and Whistler about 200 kilometres north of the city of Vancouver. They are members of the Interior Salish Indian Tribe and live on three separate First Nations' Reserves. The Lil'wat Nation lives on the Mount Currie Reserve, the N'Quatqua First Nation lives on what used to be called the Anderson Lake Band Reserve and the people of Samahquam live on the Baptiste Smith Reserve. These communities are located in the valley bottoms along rivers and lakes and at the foot of huge towering mountains. In the past the people used to travel on foot or by canoe only, later came horses, mules and oxen. When most of these people were young the only roads were the wagon trails. The railway, built in 1914, was the first modern transportation system to penetrate the area. Even now the Samahquam Reserve has to generate its own electricity and the nearest paved road is 36 kilometres away. N'Quatqua is situated on the shores of Anderson Lake at the very end of a paved road.

The memories presented with the photographs are as much as possible in the people's own words. Changes were only made to make reading easier.

May their faces and reminiscences guide us to the future.

Wim Tewinkel
February 2003

Harry Wells

Lil'wat
Mount Currie, British Columbia
Born 1928

I was at school in Mission for eight years. There were some bad times and some good times. We got quite a bit of beating when we first got there. My dad did not like me going there, because my brother died of pneumonia over there. So finally the R.C.M.P. came to take me from our house. Oh well, I did get my education anyhow.

At one time, when I was a soldier in the war in Europe, I went to set some bombs with a wire. To do that you need a timer and a box. It is just like a clock and through the electricity the bombs go off. Anyway I put that in during the night. We were stuck with a bunch of guys and the back-up that was supposed to come did not come. The Germans were all over us and the backup unit was two days late and the officer said we got to do something. I just thought I'd do it. I went right behind the German lines to set the bombs in the middle of the night. The idea was that when the bombs went off the Germans would think that they were surrounded. I had to crawl under their wires and if you touched a wire "Bang", That's it. You had to be very careful and crawl right down on the ground and you had to drag with you your own wire and the dynamite. I went by myself carrying all the dynamite, all the wires and the box. In the dark you could not see the enemy wire, but could only find it by touch and you had to be careful to touch it only lightly, so it didn't go off. When those bombs went off later that night, I tell you, the Germans just ran. They left everything. When we woke up in the morning a lot of stuff was left behind. They just ran.

A fter the bombs went off that morning there was this big guy. He comes cursing at me: " You useless siwash, don't you know where the wires are." The other guys just went after him and told him: "He put the wires up while you were asleep". That shut him up. They did give me a medal for it, but I lost it; it burned in the house fire.

S ometimes when we have a meeting I often want to tell the younger people about the old ways, but then I can't translate it into English. A lot of it is our ancestors' way. I know a lot of it, but can't translate it.

Nowadays the younger generation hardly speaks our language.

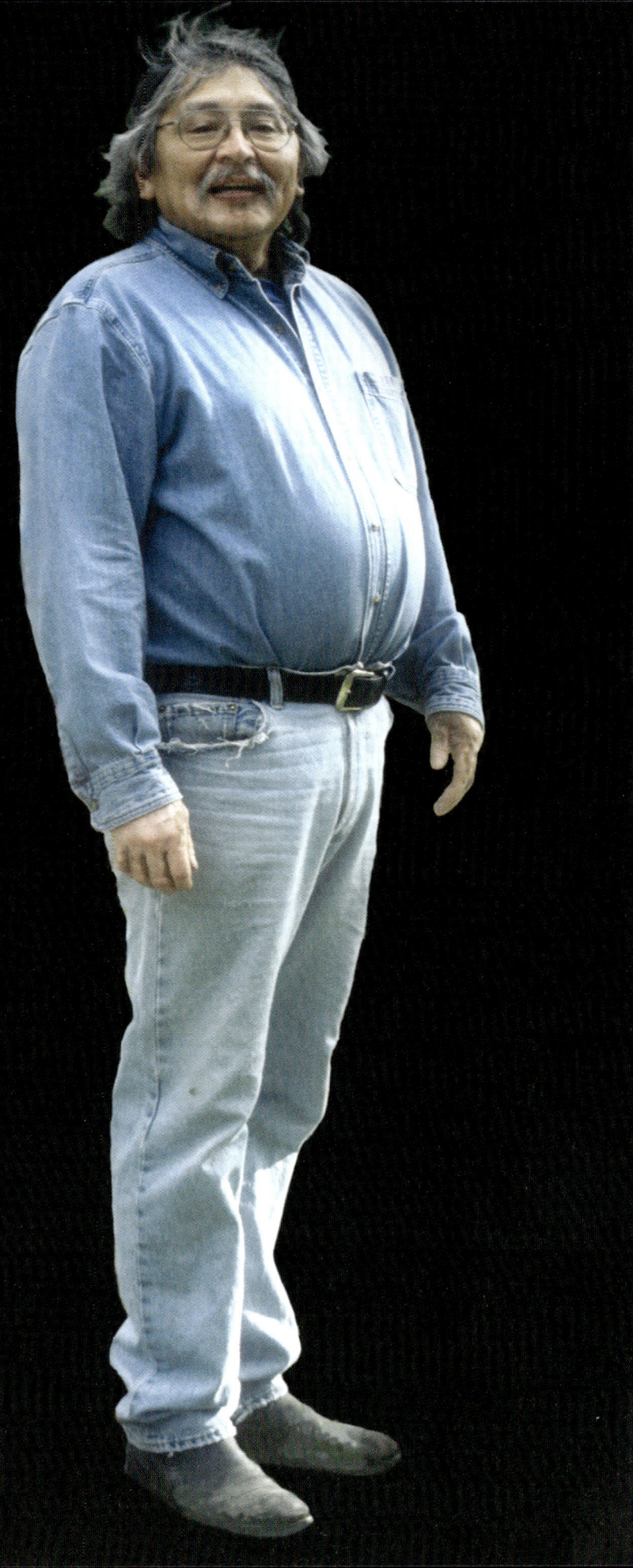

Martin Thevarge

N'Quatqua
D'Arcy, British Columbia
Born 1946

I never realized until I was older that we were better off than the people around us. We had all those cows and always had horses. My dad always worked hard to provide for us. We often ate beef and we had more than our share of deer meat.

When I was a chief in the nineteen seventies or so, my early years as a chief anyways, somehow or another I got access to the old Band Council resolutions for the powerline and the railway rights-of way. In the early days council members weren't able to write. The Band Council resolutions were all signed with an x and when I looked at them, all the x's looked the same. It looked like they were all done with the same hand by the Indian Agent or so.

On Mayday there were the horse races in Mount Currie. That was a real big event and the thing was to race the guys down there. At one time, I had a racehorse, I was sixteen, his name was Joker. I had him pulling fence wire from Elliot's Point to up here some place. We were making the range fence. I was building that fence with my dad and that is where that horse got his workout, pulling the wire. Barbed wire doesn't unroll real good, some times he would be going up a steep hill and then it would get stuck. The horse would get cross and he just jerked and he would get mad. He would run into it, you know, and it would get loose and then he would stumble. I just had the wire tied to the saddle with a rope and I would put the spool of wire between two trees on a bar.

M y earliest recollection of my childhood is standing on the porch in front of the house eating a peach and a bee stung me.

Margaret Lester

Lil'wat
Mount Currie, British Columbia
Born 1921

I got three boys and four girls. The only one not around here is my daughter who lives on Vancouver Island. She is the only one that went away. All the others are here.

I don't know anybody who in their life went through what I went through; nobody and I know everybody here. I don't have much schooling, still I am smart. I know that.

A s soon as my two boys graduated, they went to Vancouver and went back to school. I darn near died when they told me: "Mam, I am going back to school." "Going back to school" I told them, " Who is going to wake you up in the morning." That is what I used to tell them.

What I would like to know is in which year we got our first phone here in Mount Currie. I still got the same number. I never changed my phone, I never lost my phone. I used the phone lots too, because I had lots of friends all over the place. In those days it didn't cost too much money. I was the first one to get a fridge in Mount Currie. I was the first one that got a washing machine. I don't know how many I've had. I don't know how many fridges I've had. I don't know how many washing machines I've had.

Celina Stager

Lil'wat
Mount Currie, British Columbia
Born 1930

M y mother was very active. She was a leader to a lot of the women. She used to go out to check on all the elders, bath them, bring them clean clothes and help them get dressed. She used to do all that on her own time and at night anybody who was getting a baby would come and wake her up and she'd go. She would come home at any time of the night, but she never complained.

D octor Paul used to come once a month from Vancouver. He always came to our house first and Mam always had all the information he needed. She was the nurse. She had a medicine cabinet under the stairway. It was locked all the time, so we could not get into it.

My dad was chief for 25 years. I remember the days when they used to have, what they called "keet'na". When somebody got drunk and beat his wife, he had to kneel down in the presence of everybody and he would get punished, so he would not do it again. The Band had its own court. The Band was well organized. They had a chief and council and they had watchers. In those days, they had really good watchers. They were well behaved and respected. We were all in the house by nine o'clock and in bed.

My grandfather was a big chief. He was the first to ask the government for fruit trees. Everybody had big gardens, because in those days they planted lots. I know my Mam and Dad did. We had to weed, even though we were little kids and we had to pick lots of stuff. We grew cherry trees and many other fruit trees. They were all already planted before we were born.

We used to pick them and dry them. We had a big shed in the back.

We would take all the stones out of the cherries and out of the plums too and then air-dry them.

Mam had lots of chickens. She was the first one to have chickens.

We'd sell the eggs. We had cows and she used to do the milking herself. She had 7 or 8 cows. We would go early in the morning and when the pail was full, we kids used to run home to fill all the jars, then we would to go sell them for 10 cents. We all had our own customers. We would see who would sell the most, between Hilda and me and James.

Before I went to the school in Mission, I went to school here, but I learned nothing here. They called it the day school.

I went for about 6 years or so. I learned nothing until I went to Mission. There was one teacher here and when we were mad at the teacher, we all talked Indian, so he couldn't understand us. We were smart-assed some times.

There were about 60 kids in school here and just the one teacher. I did not learn anything here. I didn't know how to read here.

We never got punished severely, but the teacher used to draw an airplane on the wall and put our names upside-down falling from the plane. We had all made pictures of our selves upside down falling from the plane with our names. We didn't like that so we tried to be good. So that we did not get put up there.

When I went to school in Mission I liked sports and every Monday night, we, four girls and four boys, would go to practice. Father used to take us to Abbotsford for gymnastics courses.

We did lots of travel and when we came home, always at night time Father would take us to the kitchen for cereal. That was a treat. I enjoyed school.

Peter Williams

Lil'wat
Mount Currie, British Columbia
Born 1924

I am a military veteran of World War Two and served under Montgomery during the landing in Sicily in Italy and I remember having to wade knee-deep through waters infested with snakes. I was wounded once, but served in the war until the very end. I ended the war in Amsterdam disarming the fleeing German soldiers.

One of my most vivid memories of the war is having to shoot at young German soldiers, young kids 12 to 15 years old, that were recruited into the German Army at the end of the war.

Peter still lives in the same house on the Mount Currie Reserve, where he and his wife lived and raised six children.

Arthur Thevarge

N'Quatqua
D'Arcy, British Columbia
Born 1942

My first memory as a kid was living over here in our old log house. Just about where the cottonwoods are there.

I remember my mam and Leo the oldest of the kids, working in the garden, which was out in front of the house and the carrots were just getting ready. Leo was babysitting and he was feeding me carrots. He was shoving carrots down my throat, until my mother cried : "Leo , what are you doing." He said: "I am feeding the baby." I guess it never done me any harm and I still enjoy raw carrots.

built my house here. I must have been only 18 or 19 years old, because I started building it in 1960. It took me a long time to finish it of course. Being young you know, you don't devote all your time to it. I didn't move in until 1965. I put the roof on and just let it settle for two years, because I put two little rows of oakum between each of the cedar logs. So I put the roof on and let all that oakum settle. It settled quite a bit, because I had a wall started inside, a partition, and hell, it started to bow pretty bad and I had to take it out.

started working on the landing for my dad. He had small contract to log and clear some of the powerline right-of-way. After that he logged his own timber quota for years. He did that and then he logged for Weldwood. Eventually I graduated from bucking to driving a truck. I drove them old six by sixes; slow and hot. You just about fell asleep coming down the road with a load. The heat in the cabin was just horrendous. If you didn't stop once in awhile and get some fresh air, you'd fall asleep. We brought the logs to Devine, which was going full swing at the time.

Leslie Andrew

Lil'wat
Mount Currie, British Columbia
Born 1932

T he year I graduated, when I was sixteen, I got
a medal for the best Canadian native athlete.

I did gymnastics in school and I competed for 20 years. I started when I was a kid in the juniors. We had a team then and we trained in Vancouver at the YMCA on Burrard Street.

We use to train there after work for four or five hours. We had to practice our compulsory stuff. We competed a lot of times at UBC and for the B.C. championship and the Canadian championship. Most of the time we were in the top ten. I took parallel bars, uneven bars and rings. In my time we didn't have mats. We landed on the floor. That would hurt the feet. It was hard on the landing and you would try not to show the pain when you landed.

I left for school when I was seven. Gymnastics! That's what I liked in school.

My old coach just died not too long ago. It is about three or four years ago. He was 95 when he died.

He died of double pneumonia. He was shovelling snow in his driveway and didn't realize that snow got into his boots. I went to see him in the hospital and I asked him: "What were you doing out there. You had no business being out there. Leave it to the young kids. " All he said: "Yeah, yeah." He was from Abbotsford.

After I quit my first job in logging, I was staying at my uncle's and they asked me: " Do you still want to go back to school". I said: "Sure".

So I did carpentry. That was in November. I had nine months of extra schooling there in carpentry in finishing and cabinet making. And after that I did my apprenticeship.

Annie Jim

Samahquam
Baptiste Smith, British Columbia
Born 1908

Annie Jim is now 92 years old (2001). She had 18 children. She has now 86 grandchildren and 30 great grandchildren. She married when she was 20 years old and her youngest child was born in 1955. Her first husband was Alex Smith, who died in 1954. Later she married Mathias Jim, who died in 1994. She now lives on the Samahquam Reserve and is looked after by her granddaughters Amanda and Mona.

My dad was working in falling trees. I was born in a camp. He did a lot of falling.

I grew up in Samahquam. There is still a graveyard on the road. My dad and my mam are buried in there and so are my sisters.

In those days we used to put the butter in the water in the creek to keep it cool *(they had their own cow and churned their own butter)*. The nearest store was 30 kilometres away in Pemberton. We would hear noises at night and the next day the butter would be gone. We would find footprints and there would be an awful smell around. A Sasquatch had come and stolen the butter.

I did my own farming. I am a hard worker. If I did not work, I could not eat. We had a root cellar.

Annie Jim wirth her Daughter Rose and Granddaughter Amanda.

Annie Jim is also called Kic'ya (Elder Grandmother). Mrs. Jim has been given and owned several names, most of which she has bestowed on her daughters and granddaughters.

Rose Smith

Samahquam
Baptiste Smith, British Columbia
Born 1947

I hardly remember my dad. I do remember one time in the morning when I got up to wash my face in a basin on the floor. I had to bend down to wash my face. I had a face cloth and my dad was telling me: "This is not the time to wash clothes". He thought I was washing the clothes, but I was only washing my face as they taught us to do in school.

The sister in the school, my grade one teacher, would say: "Say your Hail Mary". I would start it in my language. They use to give us straps every time we talked in our language. Say your prayers, say your Hail Mary's. I could only say it in our language.

Sam Pascal

Lil'wat
Mount Currie, British Columbia
Borm 1925

I did not like school but I had no choice. I had to work every day, making firewood for the school. They burned wood until the school got too big then they had to turn to coal. All the older kids had to make wood by hand all the time with a handsaw.

When I came out of school there was no work. It was during the depression, so I had to learn how to trap. Later we used to make railroad ties and got two dollars a tie. We would make them with an axe, a broad axe.

Albert Thevarge

N'Quatqua
D'Arcy, British Columbia
Born 1938

They had the lodge up here, you know and tourists used to come up by train and stay here. Our dad used to get us to ride the calves so the tourists could take pictures. They used to throw coins to us mostly quarters.

I was maybe about five or six or so when I broke my arm. I was sitting on the railing and my jeans caught on a knot and when I pushed off my jeans must have ripped and I fell with my elbow on a rock and my elbow was shattered. This happened at about 11 o'clock in the morning and we could not get out with a speeder on the railroad until about 11 at night. They had a telephone line on the railroad and to make a call the speeder operator had to climb up the pole, clamp on the wires and crank up the phone before he could use it. Every so often we had to stop to check for on-coming trains. For example when we got to Seton, we had to stop there to make another telephone call. Anyway, when we got into Lillooet it was very late and dark. There was a Japanese doctor there. He grabbed my arm and I was squealing again. He had no X-ray equipment there or anything so they had to send me to Lytton and the next day we went by stage coach to the hospital in Lytton. I had to stay there all summer by myself for physiotherapy. It was a long time before I could move my arm again properly.

I did not do too well in school you know. I would have rather stayed home. I went to Mission to the school for ten years and only made it to grade six. We were pretty good at sports though. Not in basketball I was too short for that, but I was pretty good in gymnastics. One time they wanted us to go to London for the Olympics or so, but I said I would rather go home. Well, they had written my dad about it and when we got home for the summer, he was waiting at the train with a willow switch. I was the last one off the train and he had let all the others go by, so I knew it was for me.

George Leo

Lil'wat
Mount Currie, British Columbia
Born 1924

My grandfather had 20 heads of cattle and 20 horses.

After my grandparents died I was appointed to look after the farm. We shared it with the whole family. We used it mostly to grow our own food. We divided it up, except the potatoes, because that was my own hard work. I grew 5 acres a year. I lost them twice in a flood. The valley used to flood regularly, before they lowered the water level in the lake.

I remember one day when I was just a kid of about 10 years old. It was the Mayday holiday and all the people went to the dance after the horse races. They danced until the break of dawn and when they went out they saw that there was a flood. The water was right up to the last step of the hall and there was at least three feet of water. The poor guys had to wade through the water to get home to get their canoes to bring their wives home. There was three feet of water on the streets on the old Reserve.

I want to go across Canada before I am not able to walk any more. You see,

I had an accident when I was younger. A tractor I was driving rolled over. In those days there were not too many trucks around, but I had a farm and a tractor and I was hauling some wood to the sawmill.

The sawmill was across the river. They were building a bridge there and I was hauling bridge timber for this logging company with my tractor. I was going down the road and forgot to change my gear to a lower one. At that time I had already a broken leg and it was in a cast and that was the leg that you use to step on the gas. I was driving the tractor with a broken leg. I was going too fast and there was this treetop on the road. I took my foot off the gas when I saw the treetop but it was too late. My left tire hit it and the tractor rolled. It rolled on top of me and the fender was right on top of my legs. The ligaments tore. Luckily my brother was close by. He was working just across the road. I started to holler and he came running up. The tractor was already burning. There was a pole nearby that he used that to move the tractor. We were fifteen feet away and the damn tractor blew up.

My feet had been right underneath the tractor and they had to cut one of my toes off. While we were waiting for the plane to take me to the hospital, they gave me one cup full of whiskey and told me: "Down this George".

They put me in the plane and on the way to Vancouver I was singing and they were telling me: "Shut up George. Lay down". I was drunk as a skunk from that one cup of whiskey, because I was not used to drinking in those days. I guess later I must have gone to sleep again. I was for about four months in the hospital. They left the wound wide open for three months and soaked it. Every morning they packed me and soaked me and changed the dressing and then did skin grafts.

I had a horse named McKenzie King. One of the fastest on the course. They held the races usually once a year on Mayday on the 24th of May.

We used to have races on the old Reserve all the time, but then they built sidewalks of concrete and they were scared that some of our riders would be killed. So they built a racetrack.

Nick Andrew

Lil'wat
Mount Currie, British Columbia
Born 1934

First I went to school in Mount Currie, but it wasn't for very long. I guess about half a year or so. Then my brother Les came out from school in Mission for the holidays and when he was going back in September, I cried because I wanted to go with him. So finally my dad said: "You can go on the train to Pemberton and I will go and meet you there". My dad went on the wagon to Pemberton and I and my mother got on the train and we rode with Les to Pemberton. When we were about half way I was still crying, because I wanted to go. The priest came around and he asked my mother: "What is the matter with him". My mother told him: "He wants to go with his brother". So the priest said: "Okay, I will take him. If they do not want him, I will bring him back". That was the deal. Away I rode, just like a hobo. When I got to Mission, I was so happy, but only for a couple of weeks though, then I got homesick for about a week. That all happened when I was about nine years old

When I went to school, we came home for two months in the summer. My dad used to wait for us. He had a big farm and it was haying time. He used to grow a lot of potatoes and had some cattle, so he needed the hay. We had to make hay all summer.

This place was isolated for a long time. One day I went to a meeting with Chief Willie Pascal, I was one of the councillors. He told me: "You better come with me. I am going to a Chamber of Commerce meeting". During this meeting in Pemberton the subject of the road came up. There were problems with the ambulance. The only way you could get out of here was with a speeder on the railway and that took all day.

My uncle Ben was making poles across from here, where my house is now. He was hand peeling them. One day he came over and said: "Can you help me. I want to go and get my tools". I said: "Okay". So we went and harnessed up the team. We got here and my uncle said: "If I was as young as you, I'd build here". Here was the only clear spot without trees and the grass was over my head. He had me really thinking. We stopped here a few times and finally I said: "Uncle, I am going after it".

Marie Leo

Lil'wat
Mount Currie, British Columbia
Born 1922

I started making baskets when I was five or six. My mother made me start making the bottom. To make a basket you use mostly cedar roots. When you use the bark of a cherry tree you can put it in the ground for a whole year in a rusty kind of water and then it turns black or since it is red anyway, you can use it as it is. I made lots of baskets and sold them.

I was already 13 before I went to school. I went to school for three years at St. Mary's in Mission. I cried to get to school, because my parents didn't want me to go, but all my friends were going.

I enjoyed it, although I got punished a lot for not talking English. I didn't know a word of English. I didn't know how to say yes or no in English. I didn't know nothing.

I never got strapped when I got punished. They made me scrub or wash the floors. I never got strapped because I was not a bad child.

We used to go out in the bush, all the women together and if we had to stay overnight we slept under the trees. Nothing happened to us, because we talked to the animals. We picked berries and if we were looking for cedar we often would have to stay away for a few days at the time.

We had a good life on the farm. There were no stores hardly but all we needed to buy was flour and sugar. We did not miss other things because we never had them. We did a lot of hard work.

I was seventeen when I got married. I had twelve children, eight daughters and four boys. I only have Lyle left of the boys.

Alex Peters

Samahquam
Mount Currie, British Columbia
Born in 1914

I was born near Green Lake, not far from here. I was born in a logging camp. My dad was always working in the logging.

My dad was born right there where he is buried in Samahquam. Right at Samahquam at the graveyard where you turn off right on the main road.

I quit working when I turned 65. They threw me out. I was told I was too old to work in the bush, but I was still strong, when I was 65.

When I was younger, I was a logger.

I worked in the rigging, the high-rigging. Climbing trees, top them. It was a good job. You got to remember your safety that's all.

I was never scared.

You look up and decide which way the top should go, before you climb up.

While you climbed up you cleaned up the branches as you went up. So you did not get hung up.

I did it for about 20 years, then they brought in the steel towers.

I also worked on the lower Lillooet River for a couple of years, driving logs down the river. That's the most dangerous job on earth. You have to watch all the time what you are doing. You can get snagged by the logs when you work on the river. All the Peters boys used to do it.

Alex Peters,
High-rigger 1952

Alan Stager

Lil'wat
Mount Currie, British Columbia
Born in 1938

My grandfather was the Chief James Stager. He died when he was 85. My father, Alphonse Stager, became automatically Chief. My father was Chief for 25 years. He died young, he was 44 years old when he died. After he died the Indian Agent organized elections and I was elected Chief in 1972 and was Chief until 1980. After that I was a council member for awhile and I ran again for Chief in 1994 and will retire in 2003.

One summer during the school holidays I worked for the sawmill in Devine and with the money I earned I bought my first saxophone. A brand new one. I paid $ 95.00 for it. It was a tenor saxophone. That year at the school dances they let me play a few numbers with the band. I was so proud of myself, playing with the band.

started music when I went to school in Williams Lake.

They had a marching band there at the school, a very nice marching band. When I went first there and I heard them play for the first time, I got so excited. I was thrilled. I ended up playing the base drum in the marching band.

Later on we had a big bass saxophone. And then one Christmas I bought an old saxophone, a C-Melody. I brought it to Williams Lake and practiced on my own. I had those 45 records and started copying them.

Victor Smith

Samahquam
Baptiste Smith, British Columbia
Born in 1931

M y dad was sickly, he had tuberculosis and he could not work so when I came home from the first holiday from school, I was going on 13, I did not go back, because of my dad and I started to work. That was just around the end of the war in 1945.

We logged poles on the Reserve here. We got the poles out, peeled them and boomed them in the water. We would haul them up with a wagon to Lillooet Lake and put them in the water there. We would get about 400 poles per boom. Then we took them to the other end of the lake to Mount Currie, where we sold them to Osier Cedar from Bellingham. Neil Spetch, he owned the store in Mount Currie near the Reserve, was the one who trucked the poles from the lake to the railway and from there they went down. As soon as they were loaded on the railroad they were tallied and we got paid. Spetch helped us with the groceries, money, gas and everything to do all the poles. Every time we got our pay checks, when the poles were on the railroad, we didn't have very much left because of all the expenses.

We had an outboard motor then. My dad wouldn't let us use the boat for pleasure, because we needed it for the poles and if something would happen to it we would have had a hard time finding another motor. On the weekends or on days like Mayday on the 24th of May, he'd lock up the boat, so we couldn't use it. To get to Mount Currie I would take my horse and go across the river narrows here. That was before they dredged it and there was a pretty swift current. I used to go way up river and by the time we got across we were about in Mission. On the other side I'd hit the Cariboo trail all the way to Mount Currie, where I had a horse especially for the races. The trail was pretty good. About three or four o'clock on Monday morning after the dance I was back home. I used to fall asleep on the horse, but my horse was pretty smart and it would go under a tree branch that would hit me and wake me up. Then after that I wanted to stay awake so I got off the horse and hold its tail walking behind the horse all the way.

At times when the lake froze up I traveled down the other way on snowshoes all the way down to Port Douglas (56 km.), to get the things we really needed like coffee, sugar and tea. We had lots to eat from hunting and fishing and we had smoked fish and dried fish. One time I went down to Port Douglas, when there was lots of snow. I stayed on top of the snow with my snowshoes but the horse sank through, he was into it up to his chest. I pitied my horse and took my snowshoes off and walked in front of him to break his trail and then when I got tired I let him go first. We were taking turns and finally made it to Skookumchuck. There was less snow there, because there were more trees. From there on, there were lots of trees near the road and it was easier going so I could put on my snowshoes again.

Laura Purcell

Samahquam
Baptiste Smith, British Columbia
Born in 1933

My grandfather was born in the 1850's. When the gold rush came through here they hired him and he worked as water boy, traveling all over for a whole year. When he came back he spoke English and knew how to write, so they made him a chief.

I always like selling stuff. My mam said that even when I was little I used to like selling. I would grab dirty clothes and go around trying to sell it.

When I turned 16, they let me go from school. I went home to look after my brothers and sisters. I did all the cooking and everything. I did all the housework and washing the diapers. In those days they did not have throwaway diapers. There must have been half a dozen. Anyway I also worked to get a camera.

I got mail orders in from Ontario, seeds, cards and that. So I made money of those and earned myself a camera, so I could take pictures. That was in 1950 or so. I still have the pictures. The camera was a Brownie. I took pictures of all my brothers and sisters.

Morris Thevarge

N'Quatqua
D'Arcy, British Columbia
Born 1939

I was for about 6 years in residential school and two years in a day school, a public school. That was in between when I was in grade 6 and 7. The old man bought some property near Stave Lake road. He was still logging. He bought a sawmill; they were dirt cheap over there. But it did not take long to get tired of that and we all moved back. We kind of ran out of work too, there was not that much. All we could do was pick raspberries and strawberries.

At school, during the first of the year, they choose teams. When we went back to the school in September all the kids would line up and they'd get about four of the senior guys like Leslie Andrew, Oliver James and a couple of other guys and they'd all picked team members, starting with the big guys all the way down to the little guys. The senior guys would pick teams. You'd stay with that team the whole school term. We played soccer, gymnastics, track and field, all the ball games, soft ball and so on.

Everybody got a chance to play. Just when there were tournaments, when we had to go out and play other teams in the Fraser Valley they picked the best teams. Then the teams had to be the same age group.

My dad had a sawmill at Devine for a while. Right where the subdivision is now at the switchback. There are the trails all over the side hill there. That were the skid trails. He would set up the mill wherever the timber was; all horse logging. We had to build a road to haul the ties out with a little single-axle truck. We cut all the stumps down to the ground. All the sawdust went on top of the road. We usually piled the ties right beside the railroad tracks and when we had enough the inspector would come. We'd take the ones that he rejected back and mill them into lumber. We'd cut five hundred ties at a time.

Later on we had a mill at the other site of Mars' Crossing. Underneath that big fir tree that is still there. We logged out that whole area. We had to load all the ties into boxcars. All by hand. Me and Leo and a couple of other guys.

I worked for the old man for years. Five bucks a day I think. The real men were making only 8 bucks a day, a dollar or a dollar twenty-five an hour.

Bernard Dick

Lil'wat
Mount Currie, British Columbia
Born 1939

My grandparents would pick me up from my father's house. They would come down with a canoe. I would always sit in the middle of the canoe. I was really a spoiled little brat then. We would dock by the cottonwood and used a trail coming this way. Sometime we had to wade through the creek when there was high water.

I was taught how to work, so I wouldn't get lazy. I was taught to run through the river to clean my problems. I don't do that very often. I have been working since I was sixteen years old.

Song: Spirit Child

Written and composed by Bernard Dick

Spirit Child which way are you going
During the night do not lift up your child
Respect it please
A long time ago all people had believed
Never to lift up their child in the night
That they may go in the dark ways
Young Spirit Child.

The song Spirit Child is interpreted from the people's belief not to pick up kids in the night. It prescribes behaviour in the night. They were quite strict. You see a lot of difference now in the kids' behaviour.

Spirit Child is describing the way they should go.

You should not lift up your kids in the night. When I went to school we had curfew to go in at night. That is all part of Spirit Child. It is just a simple song.

Kenny Patrick

N'Quatqua
D'Arcy, British Columbia
Born 1935

I did not go to school in Mission. I went to a day school down in Texas creek near Lillooet. It was a small little log cabin and there were maybe 15 kids in school. The teacher was an Englishman by the name of Mr. Beckett. A cranky old fellow. He was very vicious. He used a three-foot ruler.

I got to about grade seven and I figured that is about all he is going to teach me. We were into geography, history and all that, and I was not a bit interested. I just said the heck with it and I went on my way. When I left there I was about fifteen years old.

I was lucky enough to work in the logging with a couple of good friends and one of them was a bulldozer operator. He ran the Caterpillar and I set chokers behind him. I used to ride back and forth with him. Sometimes he let me run the machine and after awhile I got the hang of it. And as the years went on older people that worked went on to other things and I was asked to hop right on the machine. In those days you had to have an arch behind the skidder or the Cat to keep one end of the logs of the ground.

Sometimes you had to go down the mountain with the logs behind you and once in a while you had a pretty good ride. I had some pretty good rides. I had a runaway once with a D8 Cat. We went up a draw and I had a couple of passengers with me too. They had their power saws, gas tanks and everything. We were trying to get up this spot and we just about made it to the top. We just about broken over and then the Cat started too move off the tracks. I touched the steering clutch and away she went. We must have gone down about a thousand feet or more. We bounced off a whole bunch of stumps before we got stopped. She just started spinning like she didn't have enough brakes. I put it into second gear and reverse and tried to slow her down. I had on second gear, I put it into forward and I opened the throttle right up. The tracks were just spinning, that slowed me down while we were sliding back. She slid backwards on that hill.

I did not know too much about my mother. I was adopted out right from birth and my grandmother raised me till I was 4 years old. She passed on and then my great-grandmother raised me until I was fifteen. She must have been seventy-five or eighty when I left. A real nice person, disciplined, no nonsense. There were some other grandchildren that stayed there. She looked mostly after two of us. There was a girl about 4 or 5 years older than me. And after I left my brother moved in.

FAMILY RELATIONS

Andrew, Lester – Nick and Leslie Andrew are brothers and cousins of Margaret Lester.

Jim, Peters, Smith, Purcell – Annie Jim is the mother of Victor Smith, Laura Purcell and Rose Smith. Alex Peters is her brother.

Leo – Marie Leo and George Leo are cousins.

Stager – Celina Stager and Allan Stager are brother and sister

Thevarge – Art and Morris Thevarge are brothers and so are Marty and Albert Thevarge, their fathers were brothers.